hurricane
of thoughts

category 3

by catrina

iUniverse, Inc.
Bloomington

hurricane of thoughts
category 3

iUniverse books may be ordered through booksellers or by contacting:

iUniverse
1663 Liberty Drive
Bloomington, IN 47403
www.iuniverse.com
1-800-Authors (1-800-288-4677)

Because of the dynamic nature of the Internet, any web addresses or links contained in this book may have changed since publication and may no longer be valid. The views expressed in this work are solely those of the author and do not necessarily reflect the views of the publisher, and the publisher hereby disclaims any responsibility for them.

ISBN: 978-1-4620-6081-8 (sc)
ISBN: 978-1-4620-6082-5 (e)

Printed in the United States of America

iUniverse rev. date: 10/25/2011

blackbirds fall

realize our short time is only borrowed
will we one day rise to a dark tomorrow
so many people take things for granted
from coast to coast evil has been planted

such vanity; lost in their own situation
while our planet is consumed by devastation
wars are taking so many innocent lives
without peace and love we will not survive

is anyone learning from our past mistakes
many will perish in mother nature's wake
catastrophe is facing every single soul
when will it happen no one will ever know

our society's future is so very unclear
could our worlds real end be this near
is it a sign from the clouds; a final call
from our blue sky many blackbirds fall

pale eyes

tombstone mentality; creeping thru life
struggling an emotional memory of strife
one single life disappears; a final breath
pale eyes fill with the color of death

you are dismissed

bouquet of roses; you put a smile on my face
i remember the beautiful smell died in that vase
quiet, romantic evenings spent alone at home
i had no idea my heart could turn to stone

loved the way i would dream all night about you
should have realized you could be erased too
i fell deep into the beautiful, blue of your eyes
had no clue they would ever be capable of lies

strolling all alone down our own memory lane
recalling never causing you any sort of shame
you should have never shared another kiss
finally from my life; you are dismissed

colors fill my sky

two beings sway to beauty; rhythm and rhyme

chance of true love beats in a moment of time

capturing a lost life thru a soul once dead

a sweet, tender voice that echoes in my head

the amazing color that dances in your eyes

is the same hue that fills my empty sky

point of no return

will we finally reach our point of no return

within my broken soul; my heart felt a burn

living in a hateful society with opinions so stern

in our big world; young people battle to learn

lack of love and feeding children hate on an upturn

does anyone realize what we really should yearn

will we finally reach; our point of no return

echoes of love

a summer breeze that sings with the leaves
i listen to you talk to me thru the trees
alone; i grasp your pillow so very tight
i am all yours; my heart in constant flight

thoughts of you lie me down to sleep peacefully
though you are not here; i can feel you next to me
into my nightly dreams you so eloquently dance
i can taste your kiss and our amazing romance

you are all i want and all i will ever need
it is your amazing being that completes me
roaring thru the sky; thunder in the clouds above
my soul can hear your many echoes of love

postmortem promises

a lonely, lost soul just stuck in repetitive pain
sitting beside the dry, creek bed; in search of change

your screaming and yelling ways are not my forte
how do i find a way from this horrible pain; today

name calling and untrue accusations; you are my abuse
walking on egg shells; my heart strangled by a noose

my body; your canvas painted in black and blue
what should i do; i really do love troubled you

a lonely, lost soul just stuck in a repetitive pain
sitting beside the dry, creek bed; in search of change

love is an emotion; for myself, i have been depriving
your postmortem promises; i am finally surviving

broken heart disease

beautiful, fragrant flowers i can no longer see

a shooting star; i wish you were here with me

your voice whispers love on a cool breeze

thoughts of your kiss takes me to my knees

alone; crying under a weeping willow tree

slowly dying from a broken heart disease

truth in the night

truest of love; promised under the moon
just a fairytale ending a lifetime too soon
a loving soul fell for your foolish games
constantly ridiculed by your cruel blames

my heart is as heavy as a bag of stones
without you and struggling with all alone
in search of a miracle to shed my pain
your lack of compassion drives me insane

our bedroom ceiling is slowly caving in
candles are out; my tears are suffocating
our shared affair; just doesn't seem right
your lies come like truth in the night

promise of faith

race, color, sexuality and a people that still discriminate

we continue to breed and teach our children to hate

in our cold and dark alleys the homeless try to sleep

third world countries; suffer from famine, tears weep

guns, grenades and bombs; heaven's children at war

the spiritual skies or evil hell; your decision to explore

for in a beautiful world of love we should all bathe

where souls remain surrounded by a promise of faith

neither of us walks alone

to me; you are always close and never far
do you know how marvelous you really are
every beat of my heart adores wonderful you
greatest feeling of love; no longer lost in blue

you managed to chase all my troubles away
your wonderful smile brightens my every day
softest touch that drives goose bumps across my skin
you are my true love and you have always been

those amazing eyes and the way you look at me
mesmerized by your love; this is how it should be
no longer waking to sorrows of hurt and regret
only you hold the key to the heart in my chest

you have erased the greatest pain of all
my beautiful everything; tears no longer fall
when the sun shines down upon your soul
i see two shadows; neither of us walks alone

goodbye again

before it all ends tell me where to begin
my heart breaks with your goodbye again
to give you all of me was my only notion
slowly drowning in a sea of my emotions

could have had it all but couldn't carry thru
stuck living with no chance of me and you
whispers of your love still echo thru my soul
self control; will i ever be able to let you go

falling into dark hours of sleepless nights
loneliness in search of the guiding light
before it all ends tell me where to begin
my heart breaks with your goodbye again

playing with fire

soul never to be lost in a world of submission
no hidden agenda but i am on my own mission
a new turn; it is myself i'm going to discover
do i really need and do i really want a lover

no longer do i believe in our fairytale themes
so naive to false hopes and promised dreams
a full life of happiness is my one, only desire
pay attention; you are playing with fire

my best years

no longer wanting to be lost in a simple translation
mind, body and soul in desperate need of a vacation
i wake in the earliest morning of a winter's dawn
alone; i escape to memories of where i have gone

setting aside relationships; placing them on a shelf
taking the time to find and finally discover myself
so many days pass by; yet, my heart wonders why
truest of love is so very difficult in a desperate find

a society of fools that do not know how to care
for someone; in this lifetime, i so dream to share
my unwanted feelings are ultimately in the clear
able to convert my very worst into my best years

rose colored glasses

the day we met my heart felt a love everlasting
never imagined your words and actions contrasting
i am not the one that you can walk all over
you certainly are not the world's very, last lover

my memory remembers your words of forever bliss
so frustrated and feeling like i do not even exist
our love seems to live on a lonely one way street
fell for your promise to cherish my soul for keeps

our intimacy is in a state of nothing but danger
emotions we share seems like such a stranger
your cruelty and unkindness my heart it harasses
so glad i finally shed those rose colored glasses

beautiful, white dove

a life of love is all that should be shown
hearts closed; people losing sight of your glow
daily; praying for peace and inner strength
nightly; your guardian angel visits my dreams

on our earth; pure evil and greed will rot
your words stuck in my head; i have never forgot
this shadow never, ever dances alone
wings you did bestow will help me fly home

this life you hold in your cupped hands
long time ago; a promise from a far away land
believing in your every ounce of true love
following the path of your beautiful white dove

silence in me

i hear trumpets and freedom rushes thru our wind

beautiful violins devour my soul so deep within

harps floating on clouds that pass us; goodbye

a society of black and white; we must survive

a world of peace and harmony; i hear piano keys

acceptance and love; we as a people, must see

in our faith; orchestrated thru our very being

acceptance of one another is our lives set free

erase your yesterday

just trying to erase our yesterday
i am drifting a million miles away
trying to focus on a beautiful tomorrow
a beating heart you only did borrow

in sweet dreams we once wanted to live
our beginning now lost in our own end
thoughts of you; emotions were racing
now it is closure i continue to keep chasing

a beating heart you only did borrow
trying to focus on a beautiful tomorrow
i am drifting a million miles away
just trying to erase our yesterday

mother

believing those that loved, did unconditionally
then one day those thoughts became history
all the games people play are filled with hate
struggling with an empty soul; plan an escape

pressure of life with that repeat voice in my head
many thoughts; would i be much better off dead
forget the past and bury memories; search release
thru the thundering screams i hear my peace

i thought it was right to just try and move on
precious was left behind; i was very wrong
in heartache and pain parts of me did smother
then i dried my eyes and there stood mother

day of reckoning

my cold breath on your sleeve
heart crushed under your feet
your evil lingers in my tears
allowing this feeling to last for years

letting go of your manipulating love
cruel things you did are known above
today things are going to change
one day
you will face your day of reckoning

an illusionist

always running away during times i need you most
you suck my love and i feel like only your host
you act as if your heart really does care
how could i fall into a death sentence lair

those endearing words are ever so priceless
then feelings elude you again in times of crisis
relationships will take unusual twists and turns
in times of need it is your forever love i yearn

thoughts in search of their own emancipation
time to end my suffering and character assassination
needing someone by my side always; continuous
letting you go this time; i do not want an illusionist

mr. hat

your guilty language you will never understand
false accusations, people unlike; you brand
waiting to collect things you thought you knew
a simplicity of life; you never even had a clue
the static from your soul; frighteningly familiar
find happiness within and all the rest will deliver

comfortable liar

forfeiting feelings
compromising healing
what you have done to me
down right deceiving
will not walk thru your fire
you are a comfortable liar

future shine

hopelessness; a sad spirit lost in defeat
lonely heart drowning in tears that weep
missing you; this pain takes so much time
left with scars and my own walls to climb

a horrible place i have known all too well
i am the one disgraced inside of my own hell
vicious cycle; three steps forward, six back
my mind reeling; what does my soul lack

need a fresh start; searching for a clean slate
for it is you i finally forgive; no room for hate
thoughts and bad memories i have left behind
be gone ugly past; let only my future shine

own way

from our light, society falls into darkness
people; teaching an emotion of heartless
looking for reflection in winds of direction
souls from our heaven must learn affection
yet, another beautiful day passed away
still searching and finding; my own way

love bites

the lies you so cleverly convince yourself of
how did i ever fall for you; i ask the stars above
seems you only want me for your financial gain
but i do not feel any happiness; lost only in pain

your sense of humor is more than insulting
looking in the mirror; who should i be faulting
you blow me off to run around with your friends
guess i am the one to see that what we had ends

in need of someone with a true peace of mind
you fall into the sad category of never my kind
amazing, all you want to do is argue and fight
tired of feeling this lonely emotion of love bites

a million thoughts

sadness of a heart that beats all alone
feelings and emotions remain unknown
having you; now my heart is breaking
so many tears i cry for a soul in aching

all your lies; my trust has been slain
will i ever recover from all of this pain
hiding inside the walls of my own hell
the past; my being can no longer dwell

can i survive a yesterday into tomorrow
will it be another day wasted in sorrow
burned out sun hangs in the dark sky
a million thoughts race thru my mind

you may think

you may think; i am weak but i am strong
you may think; i am lost; but, i am found
you may think; simple answers are on paper
you may think; you are right, judging wrong
you may think; righteous comes honestly
you may think; mercy street is abandoned
you may think; i am lost but i am found
you may think; i am weak but, i am strong

air in december

it is love i seek; in a desperate need to find
reminiscing memories; thought you were mine
i wander around but i'm stuck in a shell
lost in my past; left here only to dwell

my reeling emotions are so into all of you
letting you go is such a difficult thing to do
transforming pain into valuable lessons learned
peaceful future my soul really does yearn

here i stand all alone at the crossroads
which way to go; the paths covered in snow
feelings lie in black ash like burned out ember
broken heart frozen by the cold air in december

empty touch

reaching for love; shadows of empty touch
someone out there wants to share so much
total devotion and patience never torn apart
not enough time for another aching heart

all my tears dried when you came into sight
once a lonely heart; became two in flight
forever; it is your hand i swear i will hold
a beautiful story of a tale of love to unfold

your mystifying eyes clear my gray sky
a touch is all i will ever need in my life
partnership to flourish with joy; some sorrow
an ability to solve our problems by tomorrow

total devotion and patience never torn apart
not enough time for another aching heart
someone out there wants to share so much
reaching for love; shadows of empty touch

all of her good

you can hear it in the wrestling of the leaves
you can feel it on your skin in the sunset breeze
vibrant colors start to paint the pale blue sky
orange, yellow and brown fancy our eyes

a melody sung by crickets and frogs
fading with the sun; almost all gone
the fireflies no longer dance in the night
amazing change of seasons; a beautiful sight

summer's heat has finally come to pass
our colorful fall is here; finally, at last
down a path we walk and thru the woods
admiring mother nature and all of her good

my greatest pleasure

a passionate desire i have been aching for
you in my life i wanted and i got even more
your soft sweet voice is my daily serenity
my beating heart is only yours and completely

you are all the beauty my eyes can see
incredible feeling of love when you are with me
you are the reason for this smile on my face
craving your wonderful touch, a warm embrace

no pretending, this amazing life we shall share
my angel; it is you, for i will always care
it is everything you say and do, i so treasure
for you are my world; my greatest pleasure

whisper in the wind

actions excused because your heart is hurt

emotions of love to hate you easily convert

your words take their twists and turns

diminishing a chance of friendship to return

all your damage is done; period the end

a million apologies whisper in the wind

chase my yesterday

not born to walk in the shadow of a fairytale

time to take care of me; this i will not fail

family and friends; a bright future i see

being alone is where my soul lives so free

all of the hope has not been washed away

my tomorrows do not chase my yesterday

beyond measure

my heart was caged and placed on a dusty shelf
into my emotions with enthusiasm you did delve
i haven't any more room for heartbreaking pain
soft spoken words have washed away my stains

lost control of my weary soul to many tearful nights
your eyes sparkled; creating me so much delight
my perception of relationships were so confused
two people deserving of one another; finally fused

for so long; waiting for clouds of gray to disappear
you walked into my life; blue skies are finally here
a search for joy, peace, happiness and pleasure
you have shown me all of them beyond measure

crystal, clear creek flows

alone; walking down an old, dirt country road
headed to where the crystal, clear creek flows
a thousand beautiful things along the way
bright yellow sun shines down on a fall day

crisp, wind dances with the tree's changing leaves
an amazing melody sings to me in the breeze
butterflies frolic and chase with one another
like a piece of canvas creating swirls of color

bumblebees race to kiss every single flower
admiring mother nature and all of her power
boulders piled up as if in a form of defense
i just love the damaged barbed wire fence

but my favorite spot is the strange, mossy rock
the place i daydream and gather my thoughts
alone; walking down an old, dirt country road
headed to where the crystal, clear creek flows

everyday you show love

you can beat satan and his sick, evil sins
release your heart and allow all positive in
choosing to live a life of nothing but pure greed
you, alone have certainly planted the devil's seed

living in envy; your life is spent without reason
nothing good comes; season after another season
do not allow hatred toward people take control
the darkest depths of hell will own your very soul

reach out to a lonely stranger that needs a hand
to love one another, it is the our master's plan
spread love and peace throughout your own world
beautiful things will happen you never thought could

accept and believe in your wonderful higher power
all the riches of your life will flourish and flower
make it your mission to reach the stars above
this you will accomplish; if, everyday you show love

timeless thoughts

no one will understand how i really felt

flowers wilt and the snow eventually melts

for all that is left and all that i have got

is a broken heart and timeless thoughts

born to share

the western wind blows your curly, blond hair
lost time and time again; into your eyes i stare
every moment spent with you i count my blessings
the saddest of emotions; i am no longer wrestling

your soul trembling touch quenches my desire
all your loving words set my heart on fire
a warm embrace that holds my love so tight
you are the only one that has ever felt so right

dancing in my dreams nightly as i sleep
you are all i need in my life; i feel it very deep
a promise to never cause the other any despair
this beautiful life the two of us; born to share

fountain of sorrow

mind is cluttered and you can't let go

voices say you must; heart says no

can't move into a peaceful tomorrow

if you bathe in a fountain of sorrow

the midnight hour

left stranded in an unfortunate past
up to you how long the sorrow lasts
are you even able to hold the line
when you get lost in a moment of time

constant running from your problems
without a solution to solve them
do you feel like you paid the price
did others in your life also sacrifice

time to let it all go and face your fears
dry your eyes; wipe away all the tears
can you move into a new tomorrow
as the clock strikes the midnight hour

summer inman

blood of the innocent at the hands of control

evil threats take yet another precious soul

to our system that failed to protect the victim

bless you; rest in peace, summer inman

patience awaits

long, freezing nights linger forever it seems
so on days of cold i sit back and daydream
walking thru a field of fresh, growing grass
it's the best time of the year; finally at last

beautiful flowers start to bloom on trees
nectar for the taking; butterflies and bees
mighty oak and sycamore fill with leaves
silence is the sound of a soft, gentle breeze

the brook; splashing rocks, racing downstream
flocks of birds; the peaceful sounds they bring
changing of the seasons is the divine law
as winter looms; patience awaits the thaw

love and hate

a broken heart trying to get over you

daily praying for strength to get thru

to you; i was nothing but a game

your apologies are all one of the same

the false emotions are ever so cheap

all of your lies cut at me so deep

you told me i was your only soul mate

now i live on a thin line of love and hate

grave of blindness

gave it away just to have you to hold
for my own life i have lost much control
falling in love; the worst thing i could do
lessons learned were all because of you

slipping even deeper into a black hole
sadness and frustration took its toll
my emotions all your words did rape
caught in a hell; can i find my escape

the innocence had fled my soul
no choice but find my way back home
thru faith i found a world of kindness
hard i experienced; a grave of blindness

set fire to memories

thought you were the best thing in my life
everyday the sun still shines very bright
so the person you claim; you cannot be
the rivers eventually meet the blue sea

your love once filled all my empty space
spring days; butterflies still frolic and chase
your many lies took away all of my pride
daffodils still bloom upon the countryside

loves end; searching for rhyme and reason
trying to escape my unhealthy, mad season
nothing left to remind me of how you hurt me
yesterday i set fire to all of our memories

i want to believe

i want to believe; all your words are true

i want to believe; you will never leave me blue

i want to believe; that i am your everything

i want to believe; your emotions are genuine

i want to believe; you will hold me very dear

i want to believe; you will always be there

i want to believe; you will cherish my heart

i want to believe; you will never, ever part

i want to believe; i am all your eyes see

i want to believe; you really do love me

i want to believe; i want, to believe in you

yellow raincoat

stuffed into a red, white and blue tote

with a fake smile and a shade of gloat

into the wind our society cast a vote

shocked; when promised words choke

speeches lost in translation of no hope

in skies of gray; i wear a yellow raincoat

i carry pride

for this is my life i was only born to live
promise from my heart it is compassion i give
choice is preached; at a cracked mirror i stare
feelings no one understands nor do they care

you can hear it in my voice; i need the truth
i have nothing to hide but so much to lose
knowing that i was different for many years
even behind the mask i taste my own tears

as long as i show only love and never hate
this life i will live will be nothing but great
dark corner i cower alone; soul lost inside
for i am a normal human being; i carry pride

no bravery

heart breaks; unable to decide what to do
your quality of life is solely left up to you
natural caregiver but losing sight of yourself
friends sympathize and offer all their help

everyday; should you stay or should you go
gut tells you your life is not someone's show
searching for acceptance to fill low self-esteem
lost in a controlled life that has no meaning

so afraid of change; will you succeed or fail
stepping stones are laid; follow the right trail
caught in your own life's codependent slavery
unable to escape; living daily, with no bravery

painful day in july

believed in a life shared between you and i

there was a time your love made me high

now; i'm so tortured by your despicable lie

blood shot, swollen eyes do nothing but cry

every single day; pieces of my heart die

and my days of pain fill my once, blue sky

just cannot stop asking myself; why, why

i have no choice but to bid you goodbye

you were my most painful day in july

depths of my soul

there is no breath left inside my soul
everyday i cry and try to let you go
heart will never heal; so mangled
with thoughts of you; lost and tangled

tears just weep down my cheek
once a true love; always for keeps
you promised me forever and a day
how could you just walk away

trying to sleep; i grip your pillow tight
left here all alone every single night
fighting dark hours; you enter my dreams
i get lost in our wonderful memories

trying to come to terms that we are done
how will i survive without the one i love
i will never, ever be able to let you go
this i promise from the depths of my soul

sweet revenge

it is all of the evil you choose to delight
a life of wrong doing; you were never right
with a plan in motion, no matter how insane
on a mission to hurt and cause others pain

playing the victim is ultimately your sad story
always living in a heartless moment of glory
lacking human compassion with a heart so cold
a broken soul so alone left to grow very old

lies, manipulation, deception; your daily ways
there lives a powerful force that will have a say
she creeps by night; left to make a soul cringe
karma; she is the only silent, sweet revenge

behind your shadow

every single day is covered with a slow rain

such a wasted life of heartache and pain

still living off all your dirty, little secrets

consumed by your extra baggage of regrets

unable to figure out a future that is unclear

so lost in an ache of wish you were here

you feel like you have no where to go

you must stop living behind your shadow

paper moon

the paper moon hangs bright in our dark sky
you stare at it every single night and ask why
so many moments that you can never take back
each one of the lies spread like concrete cracks

two, innocent broken hearts; shattered and torn
some days you wish you had never been born
now it is only loneliness that consumes your soul
silence all around as you sit upon a grassy knoll

hurt and pain caused by your deceitful ways
to the love above; for forgiveness you pray
the paper moon hangs bright in our dark sky
you stare at it every single night and ask why

in the meadow

lonely harp plays in the meadow

orchestrating our future
shadows so trapped
world without compassion
a pat on the back
without a hand to give

lonely harp plays in the meadow

your goodbye

my aching heart bleeds dry
without your love my tears cry
repetitive words; your goodbye

no one will ever take your place
in my misery and sullen disgrace
i search for the smile on my face

on my lips it is only you i crave
still missing you every single day
my own lonely life left in dismay

together; i wanted us to grow old
instead my dreams are left so cold
the pain just grows within my soul

my aching heart bleeds dry
without your love my tears cry
repetitive words; your goodbye

silhouettes and memories

in every single cold, empty room
i can still see your shadow move
with your manipulation, cheating and lies
you live in a masquerade of disguise
our love you did not even share
feeling as if you really never cared
every night i hear your heartbeat
alone i lay visiting you in my dreams
dancing with you one last time
silhouettes and memories in my mind

if only

if only
you heard the way your words manipulate
if only
you were aware evil makes your soul debilitate
if only
you could see how all of your lies cut so deep
if only
you realized it is drama you continue to feed
if only
you could conceive that you live in a sad song
if only
you could distinguish between right and wrong
if only
you understood these things keep you lonely

if only

path i chose

searching for my freedom's destination
tired of living with so much frustration
ghosts creep in from a saddened past
to forgive and forget; finally, at last

the heart that beats inside my chest
is the only one i do not second guess
a wasted life spent chasing lost loves
beautiful family sent from heaven above

day after day just trying to stay strong
blood thicker than water it's been all along
the softly, lit lantern shows the way
down the only path that i chose today

see you smile

i love your amazing, positive attitude

i love your wonderful spirit; never rude

i love the way the wind blows your hair

i love the happiness you and i share

i love your mesmerizing, blue eyes

i love the way your hand fits in mine

i love the way your heart is so caring

i love all the memories we are sharing

i love the way you make my butterflies race

i love that no one will ever take my place

i love your beautiful, expressive style

most of all; i love to see you smile

last lullaby

speak of compassion but your words are fake

cruel tongue and another innocent heart breaks

such a shame your personality is so shallow

in the dark you dance with your own shadow

where is all of the promised style and grace

from my soul and memory you will be erased

it is the truth that exists in all of your lies

yesterday; i had listened to your last lullaby

false promise

friendship; should exist with a conscience

tasting all of the hidden clues in darkness

in my lover; you have developed a fondness

i now vow to feed my very own soul solace

as i try to swallow; your false promise

crucible of carnage

best in the world without a heaven; carry too much pride
wheel for where you will be broken; you are unable to hide
are you jealous of others fortunes; so green with envy
within freezing water your soul for eternity shall be living
desire more than what you need; so consumed by gluttony
force fed rats, toads and snakes; and the rest is history
was it an act of procreation or did you commit just lust
smothered in fire and brimstone for a breach of trust
facade that you speak only love; hurt, you opt for anger
alive; limb by limb you will be torn; no escape from danger
do you desire material wealth or gain; an obsessive greed
soul in oil you shall soak and boil; money is the evil seed
dancing through life looking for hand outs; lazy as a sloth
snake pit you shall dwell in hell and this will never stop
did you live all your life walking on at least one edge
do you think your soul will survive a crucible of carnage

my kind of wonderful

you remind me of a thousand beautiful things
so grateful you flew into my life on angel wings
finally my broken emotions your kindness did repair
mesmerized with the constant laughter we share

your amazing personality keeps me warm everyday
your gorgeous, blue eyes sparkle and light my way
each time you touch me it makes my butterflies race
you alone have placed a permanent smile on my face

with an unselfish caring way; you reign supreme
i carry your warm embrace into my daily dreams
you have no idea how you complete my soul
you are my one and only; my kind of wonderful

creek side

alone; sitting by the creek side
simple pleasures; silence of nature
gazing at the beautiful, blue sky
absorbing the bright, golden sun
the leaves wrestle with the wind
many colorful flowers in bloom
scent of summer rides the breeze
clear water racing down stream
life found in a monarch butterfly
tranquility of serenity and peace
alone; sitting by the creek side

beautiful disaster

walking alone under the city lights in the pouring rain
clouds shuffle across the sky; reminiscing my pain
new love; two people set out to seek and discover
butterflies and goose bumps made us perfect lovers

how did i get lost in the magic of your disguised eyes
my soul poisoned and devastated by daily promised lies
plainly i remember that day i begged you not to leave
i am shameless; finally, picking myself up off my knees

as thoughts of you enter my mind; night rushes into dawn
hidden emotional scars; my love, i am no longer your pawn
it was my heart and feelings for which you did master
you ended up being nothing more than my beautiful disaster

memory of a dream

tears dance in memory of a dream

seems; commitment meant forever

clever; you and the deceitful game

same; i swear to never, ever be

history; is where you shall lay

today; i finally found my soul in me

dream; you escaped my memory

full length mirror

convinced by lies; it is drama you create
stirring innocent people in a frenzy of hate
so lost in the games you play so very well
then you pass the collection plate to hell

you sit and manipulate; messing with minds
like a plague, you destroy the lives of kind
selfish thoughts; think you are in the clear
seek true reflection in your; full length mirror

excuse

an excuse; is what you abuse
is this the life that you choose
in shadows of hate, you accuse
no real love; thru life you cruise
your comprehension is abstruse
suffocating all but you; by a noose
your sad soul later searches truce
papers read; tomorrow, old news
your excuse; is what you abuse

seasons change

acting like you are a kind and gentle soul
shocked at the real you that finally unfolds
manipulating ways light up your evil eyes
you just love being the master of many lies

finally caught up in all your scheming turmoil
playing the victim; all your games are foiled
stopped dead in your tracks; from eyes tears cry
grasping for attention; creating your own demise

unable to focus on true friendships that mattered
responsible for your own image you shattered
your personality never, ever stays the same
just like the way all of the seasons change

healing fate

many of the people kneel to pray

even all of the hypocrites that betray

heaven's plan; no, i don't think that it is

to do people wrong and ask for forgiveness

are you inevitably ready for a powerful wrath

will we drown in our very own blood bath

living in a world of so much hate

guiding light should be our healing fate

fireflies and mudpuddles

thinking of such a wonderful childhood; i find chuckle

many hours spent chasing around escaped bubbles

on sand surrounded by castles, buckets and shovels

forts with pillows, blankets and crawl thru tunnels

catching fireflies at sunset when the day finally settles

refreshing, spring rain brought pies from mud puddles

buried in milk; i loved the soggy, cookie crumbles

back then the woods sure seemed like a huge jungle

beautiful picture unveiled upon completion of a puzzle

thinking of such a wonderful childhood; of no troubles

finally found you

i am trying to learn to live all over again
my heart aches and is tainted by past sin
myself, i have lost; happiness i need to find
deafening silence; rising is my darkest sunshine

another beautiful day passes by; twilight looms
hurt haunts like a ghost; lost in eternal gloom
running out of tomorrows; meaningless time
pain keeps repeating without reason or rhyme

tripping over bitterness of saddened memories
craving to meet someone that is just like me
i thought sharing my love was forever through
until that amazing day; i finally found you

treasured image

with an emotional tribute; push, pull, shove
a lack of compassion and a facade of love
lies, manipulation and your deceitful way
you are nothing like the person that you say

all of the greed does not buy you happiness
one day you will rise to a life of scantiness
witness to your karma will be a privilege
and forever in my mind; a treasured image

sunday song

hidden under your white cloak
lost; still searching for your hope
baptized in the holy water
do you live a life of falter

do you follow a belief of hate
standing in the line of discriminate
some loathe your organized religion
along with your final decision

evil absorbs your hypocrisy
believing you live in harmony
does it sustain you all week long
can you live by the sunday song

barely breathe

i can barely breathe
this day has set on me

on a cloud i want to ride
to feel our feelings inside

moon replaces the sun
what i have done

this day has set on me
i can barely breathe

change

impaired; i stand all alone
struggling to find a way home
from my feelings; i estrange
my soul must accept change

drift away with you

here is where you and i can finally be free
on the old tire swing we fly as high as can be
in our imagination everything is so sweet
soft blades of grass tickle our bare feet

along the creek; we walk hand in hand for miles
bright, yellow sun shines down on shared smiles
escape from reality only belongs to you and me
summer breeze dances with all the tree's leaves

so much beauty; everyday seems you are queen
butterflies play with daffodils in a valley of green
a safe place where nothing hurts, never at all
fresh smell of a misty rain from our waterfall

heaven of no hate and only love is forever true
plaid blanket and a romantic picnic for two
white, puffy clouds float by in a sea of blue
into our daydream; i drift away with you

love should

love should come easily
honestly
if your soul does believe

from the darkness to light
feelings; we take flight

love should come honestly
easily
if our souls do believe

no guarantee

stepping into a future of no guarantee
our days are filled with uncertainty

to a life of lonely; my soul is chained
causing myself much unnecessary pain
my empty heart beats thru my veins
i should not treat my past like a stain
it is only, my happiness that remains
peace of mind; i want to truly attain

our days are filled with uncertainty
stepping into a future of no guarantee

thunder in the valley

each season serves us a magical purpose
eventually; all new life will finally surface
buried under a blanket of fallen snow
from brown to green; our grass will grow

heavens creatures, ready to escape freeze
rain feeds colorful blooms on our trees
a light breeze fills the air with country
soon; a search for clovers, that are lucky

petals of shades of yellow, catch the eye
and our stars have escaped the gray sky
just a witness to mother nature's finale
i lie down listening to thunder in the valley

lips of an angel

your creations wake us with your amazing song

beautiful melodies that teach us right from wrong

white, puffy clouds float across your blue sky

bright, yellow sun shines peace upon every eye

life you breathe to every single boy and girl

even your miracles as small as an oyster pearl

so full of happiness a heart begins to swell

words of love whispered from lips of an angel

language of love

our magic sparks a bright, brilliant fire
a beautiful feeling two hearts so desire
you have set my emotions in full swing
in my heart you are my only everything

finally; the truth is so very plain to see
within your arms i know you cherish me
our marvelous future dances in brisk air
breathing in every single thing we share

my amazing day starts with your smile
forever; hand in hand we walk for miles
soft words whispered across your tongue
i am mesmerized by your language of love

shadows of mistakes

the yellow lights the blue sky
single tear streams from my eye

searching daily to just find cope
seems i prayed for my last hope
how long does it really take
to learn from shadows of mistakes

cocaine lined on a piece of chrome
all alone; the streets i call home
too many years; lost in my history
society and all the jealous misery

the yellow lights the blue sky
single tear streams from my eye

inviting disease

should i free fall into your lies and deception
everyday; i wait for your ugly transgression
i will never be angry; if you really only knew
the truth, in your own misery; i will take in lieu

who lives a life without any sort of sacrifice
your hurtful words turn my heart into ice
trying to search for your truth; in your misery
can't you see; drama is an inviting disease

silent dawn

a heart left with a weak beat
tear of hurt rolls down my cheek
disappointed in my very own hostility
actions are solely my responsibility

thoughts of lessons taught young
words can hurt with a sharp tongue
i will not dance in an empty ballet
coming winds will wash the pain away

lying in a yawl beneath the mizzen
stars finally sleep beyond the horizon
running away; now i am withdrawn
sun rises within the silent dawn

ruins

living in your own world of disbelief

a different color; changing like a leaf

your attitude of a me, me syndrome

it will leave you eventually; all alone

blaming others and anything less human

you will stumble thru your own ruins

wilted veins

sun will set; a shadow of lost souls remain
thru days of change our world is insane
our beings swelter; will we ever be the same
a lost, savage soul; rips thru our wilted veins

only an emptiness

from the start; it was a friendly card read
playing with emotions of true love; mislead
thoughts race thru my lost, weary mind
are you a commitment turned an evil blind

your promises leaving on a breath of lies
for far too long myself has been on standby
selfish actions that strike a soul with deadliness
your wide, open arms offer; only an emptiness

old hay wagon

growing up as children we would tend to the cattle farm
moments and nature's charm; reflecting on years gone
calendar passed us by and the season's changed
many of all our daily chores remained the same

water and feed the animals at dawn and at dusk
both parents worked; for us kids this was a must
big field seemed a million acres back in the day
there's the old wagon; seven high and a tie of hay

hammer and nails; can't even count the times we mend fence
oh and that evening all six of us had to catch the escaped pigs
during the fall; inside the huge, unused, corn crib walls
working as a team; we would stack firewood so tall

i remember the day our parents sold; i just cried
made my way to the barn loft and stared at the blue sky
our memories will always be and we lived in this world
but you can never take the country out of the girl

painful memories

in a corner i cower; haunted by my shadow of darkness

struggling to reach my life's destiny of a calmness

seems i have been drowning in my tears for centuries

a weary, desolate soul trying to escape painful memories

restart

walking on a lonely avenue of broken dreams; i restart
suffocating on the smoke from my burning heart

my vision is blurred as tears fill pails with my pain
comfortable in your victim game; you always place blame
deceitfulness that cut the blood of love from my veins
with crippling lies; you alone, our trust has now been slain
casual manipulations; positive, from my soul you did drain
eventually; all of these scars will fade from your stain
like a huge, black hole of evil; from you i must constrain

suffocating on the smoke from my burning heart
walking a lonely avenue of broken dreams; i must, restart

dawn's dusk

living a life on the other side of nowhere
preying on kindness of others; like you care
the night falls and all is quiet and calm
suddenly, drama explodes like a time bomb

soulless with your evil, manipulating ways
causing innocent lives heartache and pain
making up lies to hurt people's feelings
left only to suffer from your cruel dealings

many friends are fighting; lovers are crying
laughing; a sly, quiet way you slip into hiding
releasing you from our lives is such a must
memories of you will disappear in dawn's dusk

shadows dance

struggling daily; fighting my fall into relapse

upon a bed of nails my soul has collapsed

the pain of a lost love is so hard to swallow

your deceitful ways has left my heart hollow

why did our shared love have to slip away

if i could do it again; i would save that day

heartless lie that erased our second chance

within my many tears your shadows dance

anatomy of peace

forgive and forget; never, ever live in the past
it will resolve the heart of conflict; at last
always smile at a stranger every single day
you'll be amazed at good that comes your way

always tell the truth even if the truth hurts
by now you should know even a white lie is worse
lend a hand to someone who is down on their luck
someone will pay it forward when you are stuck

respect another opinion even if you don't agree
all different walks of this life can make history
always walk a mile in someone else's shoes
doing this you will experience a different bruise

wake every single day and appreciate your life
eventually it will come natural without even a try
your soul will fill with big love at the very least
short life we live; live it with an anatomy of peace

soul crawls

in an evil world you live to leave innocent bleeding

with all the hateful that boils in your selfish being

trying to understand; how you think you do not sin

my soul crawls; suffering beneath my torn, skin

turn the page

we are all eventually judged by our heaven's divine
enjoy your wonderful life; it's a race against time
there are many days our lives bring us much pain
even some of the moments we must accept change

walk away from those that stab you in the back
revenge is never a solution; there will be an attack
acceptance and love is every persons yearning
by the trials and tribulations we keep on learning

all of our days dissolve at every midnight hour
living in the past will cause your tomorrow to sour
don't live this one chance life in a constant fit of rage
take a very, deep breath and just turn the page

thousands of lies

the earthquakes are shifting our big world
prophecies; are they our real end, unfurled
tsunamis sweeping the living out to sea
society in denial; this can't happen to me

over sized hail sent from the clouds above
falling upon people who forgot how to love
marine life dies at the hand of an oil spill
how can so much greed offer any goodwill

so many souls will live in a grave of pain
and our dark skies will fill with fire and rain
from a dawn, the mighty divine will rise
truth will come for the thousands of lies

infatuation

everyday; beautiful you at the train station

i drift into such a wonderful state of elation

your eyes and smile paint my imagination

your smell; like you bathed in carnations

the caress of your skin is my temptation

you fill my soul with astonishing admiration

without a touch; you tickle my sensation

only a divine angel; heaven's creation

unrequited love; left in my own frustration

in my dreams; you will always be infatuation

days of requiem

blue skies turn to a fierce black; mile wide funnel forms
destroying everything in its path and leaving people scorn
foot by foot a freight train breeds in our own tainted seas
timeless catastrophic sweep; our lands littered with debris

our very planet's core is boiling; a violent anger erupts
ash fills the air we breathe to a weak society; so corrupt
wildlife, timber, farm land destroyed; such a slaughtering
bright flames like our hell; just a trail of burnt offerings

from a love we stem and now we mourn all over again
same story taught for years but some have chosen sin
thoughts and prayers; all across our small world it seems
have we reached our end in an unwanted days of requiem

beneath the skin

beneath the skin
lies all of our sins
manipulation and deceit
leaving; unfortunate weak

things are not right today
to our knees we must pray
beneath the skin
lies all of our sins

violent rhythm

portraying you; an energetic personality of winsome

with an ode to love; you promised us a kingdom

for i no longer know me and who i have become

living every minute in a confused state of fearsome

many years i have suffered you; my ailing symptom

i must escape your world; my life as your victim

your words cut so very deep with a violent rhythm

moving picture

do not lie; allow truth to be your guide
behind rumors you should never hide
you must not regret; if, to out live your past
forgive and forget; all evil will be outcast

never, ever wish ill will upon another soul
after all; a peaceful afterlife is your goal
appreciate every one of heaven's creations
and fill the world with much adoration

follow all the rules from the sky above
remember, your day will come; to be judged
every choice we make dictates our future
days of our lives; merely a moving picture

your own darkness

within your cold, evil soul; hatred is creeping

hurting others and leaving hearts bleeding

how will happiness in my being really exist

it is your negative energy; that i will desist

all alone with your conscience of heartless

is it very lonely living in your own darkness

the black suitcase

the black suitcase is packed and we try to move on
from the ones that loved us; we have withdrawn
wild and very free; we can only see a future bright
on our own we thought our days would be all right

meeting liars, users, mental and physical abusers
every where you turn seems there's another loser
adolescence taught us to love every boy and girl
but; how do you escape the weight of the world

our familiar roads that help us back to our home
returning down the same path we've always known
from all the ones that hurt us; we have withdrawn
the black suitcase is packed and we must; move on

heavenly days

my soul disappeared into lonely; grasping fear
thinking to myself, my end is very clear
waging war with broken thoughts in my head
a lifeless soul; feelings are so torn and dead

drowning quickly in puddles of my fallen tears
life so sad; trying to survive without you here
your cruel intentions were as cold as ice
should've known; been thru this at least twice

i've been searching for love for far too long
with someone special i want to share my song
i struggle and ponder my heartbroken sorrows
connecting the puzzle pieces for a new tomorrow

time is the only key to setting myself free
pulling myself together; missing the real me
i am only my master; no longer your slave
faith; i will grow stronger for heavenly days

a dream

drifting all alone in the damp darkness
pulling me closer as if with a harness
the sound of fallen leaves under my feet
caught in a nightmare; lost in defeat

wondering thoughts flowing aimlessly
ahead my weary eyes see part of my history
mostly flashing before me; good deeds
there were days anger owned my being

searching for palpitations within my chest
must be dead; this is my only guess
voices cackle and howl from a black corner
this is it; soul left in an eternity of horror

a single, solitary tear runs down my cheek
falling fast and my body feels so very weak
waking to a beautiful sunrise and silent screams
gasping for air; it was nothing more than a dream

pieces of me

true happiness disappeared like a ghost
i left me when i needed me the most
trying to find the place that i belong
relationships ending in such a sad song

different kind of love; ready for the chance
this single heart to beat in a new dance
the long search for tranquility i did find
leaving some pieces of me behind

a beautiful favor

living at the fault of an alibi, that; you did buy
all the evil you harbor is lost in a paper doll lie
manipulating souls is your greatest pleasure
thunder rolls and the dark offers you a treasure

trapped in games you played; drowning in sorrow
gasping for a last breath; searching for tomorrow
without you; my life gained much more than greater
and the day you left, was; a beautiful favor

embrace the passion

a kind word or a smile can make a person's day

forever; not one soul should you ever betray

giving is to open new doors to your receive

in a faith to do only right you must believe

always appreciate many beauties in our world

we are all just merely a vulnerable boy or girl

to love one another is never out of fashion

allow your inner self to embrace the passion

midnight rain

just lying here in puddles of my own pain
missing minutes of my life; ticking away
living in shadows of mistakes i've made
i could not control the way you behaved

beautiful, free, falling waterfalls freeze
stillness of a soul; a drop to weary knees
listening to raindrops tap the window pane
it is time to dance in the midnight rain

meant to be

you are so lost and out of our sight
your presence is felt here every night
loved by many and an aspiring teen
young girl, jaded; caught in between

less active in the dawn of our day
so sad your life has been taken away
scared without any emotion; facing fear
where your soul will linger for years

so the saying goes; the good die young
follow the light; head toward the sun
natalia; set your beautiful soul free
a guardian angel you are meant to be

standing tall

road to recovery; in search of my home
looking for a life to call my very own
caught by the lies that left your lips
an illusion of love for i did not wish

all the evil things that your soul did do
every one of them are going to haunt you
all the years i believed your pretending
your deceitful ways i am remembering

the cold, dark, lonely days no longer rise
all of my amazing dreams of us; goodbye
for your emotional madness i refuse to fall
my everlasting faith keeps me standing tall

my final chapter

i miss your laughter every single day
way you made me smile and the things you'd say
entangled in a dream of just one more kiss
the words i love you whispered from your lips

my soul aches and this broken heart moans
you are gone; this house is no longer a home
i sit all alone in this melancholy place
every time i close my eyes i see your face

my precious time seems to just stand still
without you i want to die; it is my free will
for us there will be no happily ever after
writing of a lost love; my final chapter

runaway freight train

runaway freight train runs thru my weary head
my heart skips a beat and i feel like i am dead
running in circles; an overgrown field of lost souls
who holds my future; who ruined my goals

agony and suffering claim my soul; set me free
rusty, linked chains drag; creeping behind me
in the cold, dark distance i hear a crow's cry
bloody tears seep from my obstructed eyes

lingering beyond my body covered in a sheet
staring at the heavens above; prayers i repeat
seasons change and i experience the same pain
goodbye; as i step into a runaway freight train

touch of your skin

within my dreams is where all your beauty lies

when i need comfort; i get lost in your eyes

all my mornings start with your amazing smile

the scent of you engulfs me like lily of the nile

with you is where my heart has always been

everyday; i still crave the touch of your skin

our steep cliff

all i feel inside is sadness and sorrow
my love; all you wanted was to borrow
by the roaring ocean tides i just sit
this time; high atop our steep cliff

i lie awake dreaming; absorbing all darkness
all of the manipulating and deceit was heartless
lightning bolts stretch down from the sky
arms drawn in the air; please tell me why

like a cold, rainy mist my blue eyes cry
in a fog your tempting lips are disguised
the truth; you never had a simple clue
it's time for you to face the ultimate truth

all i feel inside is sadness and sorrow
my love; all you wanted was to borrow
by the roaring ocean tides i sit
this time; high atop our steep cliff

antique cracked mirror

my dreams went up in smoke the day you left
like paper and fire i was choking on death
sitting amidst wilted flowers and fallen leaves
birds sing filling my soul with sad memories

ambition and hope has escaped my desire; life
emotional whirlwind falling into pitfalls of strife
thru seasons searching for self preservation
for i will not be with another; never a relation

years pass; still lonely, from swollen eyes i cry
no chance of return; my own life passed me by
reflection of saddened pain still shows on my face
antique, cracked mirror hangs in the same place

wishing upon a star

you turn away and we slowly drift apart
feeling the weight from heaviness of the heart
aching pain in my chest beats with persistence
my silent screams echo with such impatience

it is a mystery why i must have you with me
gasping for the tainted air we use to breathe
all of your pernicious words drive me insane
why would you inflict upon me so much pain

white roses are wilted; us, you never did cherish
for with time; my memories of you i hope perish
you are so close to me yet so very, very far
to the heavens i stare; wishing upon a star

seduced by your lies

stuck on your words that were so very truthful
spoken without any feeling; could i be the fool
emotions poured out on the love notes you sent
leaving all my deep feelings broken and bent

wanting to touch me much longer than a while
each morning i wake to shadows of a fake smile
beautiful sounds of love whispered from your lips
my soul poisoned from yet another tainted kiss

showed me the sunshine when skies were stained
never thought you would return the same pain
causing so much sorrow and tears within my eyes
allowing my own heart to be seduced by your lies

knock at your door

all different walks of life struggle in a whirl

we are all children of this beautiful world

to really love one another is not a chore

do not allow hatred to knock at your door

next message

parading around yourself; dancing in a false facade
your actions, manipulations and lies are not so odd

next message

politicians making our laws; acting like rebellious children
teaching all of our innocent, that morals are forbidden

next message

our entertainment is filled with filth; sexual driven minds
how in a world of deceitful can we build a world of kind

next message

struggles will continue and the hate will eventually prevail
hypocrisy; i will not fall, i am constantly learning to exhale

next message

life of a marionette

i have traveled all the way around the globe
from egypt to italy and all the way back home
i can entertain many; from the young to the old
i even performed in a shakespeare sold out show

once a star in the christian church morality plays
a sense of humor; banned i am, still to this day
you can clearly see the smile on my wood face
guaranteed to be laughing when you leave this place

i can tell a good joke; i can even sing and dance
pull up a chair; sit back relax, give me a chance
unable to move; in this black box i just lay
waiting for my manipulator to come out and play

the list

to accept all things can and will change
to learn to live without any sort of blame
to help a stranger in desperate need
to smile at someone you never did meet
to learn everything happens for a reason
to appreciate every changing season
to never wish ill will upon any enemy
to always, always love unconditionally
to be a good sport even if you win or lose
to know everyone lives the way they choose
to realize all people are born with an opinion
to know this life is meant for only living
to learn nothing is gained living in the past
to know money never, ever buys happiness
to learn you are never lonely with a family
to always know karma can be an anomaly
to know if someone does not like you; their loss
to learn to never hate anyone at all costs
to know you are responsible for what you do
to learn it is important to forgive too
to know that all cruel and evil words hurt
to learn to appreciate this beautiful earth